N. Scott Momaday

ANGLE OF GEESE AND OTHER POEMS

David R. Godine

TO CAEL

David R. Godine Publisher
Boston, Massachusetts

LCC 73-84886
ISBN 0-87923-085-1

'The Bear,' 'Buteo Regalis,' 'Pit Viper,' and 'Earth and I Gave You Turquoise' first appeared in the *New Mexico Quarterly;* 'Simile' in *Sequoia;* 'Before an Old Painting of the Crucifixion' and 'Angle of Geese' in *Southern Review;* and 'Headwaters' and 'Rainy Mountain Cemetery' in *The Way to Rainy Mountain.*

Designed by Carol Shloss

Number 5 in the
FIRST GODINE POETRY
CHAPBOOK SERIES

Jan Schreiber, General Editor

Angle of Geese

The Bear

What ruse of vision,
escarping the wall of leaves,
rending incision
into countless surfaces,

would cull and color
his somnolence, whose old age
has outworn valor,
all but the fact of courage?

Seen, he does not come,
move, but seems forever there,
dimensionless, dumb,
in the windless noon's hot glare.

More scarred than others
these years since the trap maimed him,
pain slants his withers,
drawing up the crooked limb.

Then he is gone, whole,
without urgency, from sight,
as buzzards control,
imperceptibly, their flight.

Buteo Regalis

His frailty discrete, the rodent turns, looks.
What sense first warns? The winging is unheard,
Unseen but as distant motion made whole,
Singular, slow, unbroken in its glide.
It veers, and veering, tilts broad-surfaced wings.
Aligned, the span bends to begin the dive
And falls, alternately white and russet,
Angle and curve, gathering momentum.

Pit Viper

The cordate head meanders through himself:
Metamorphosis. Slowly the new thing,
Kindled to flares along his length, curves out.
From the evergreen shade where he has lain,
Through inland seas and catacombs he moves.
Blurred eyes that ever see have seen him waste,
Acquire, and undiminished: have seen death –
Or simile – come nigh and overcome.
Alone among his kind, old, almost wise,
Mere hunger cannot urge him from this drowse.

Comparatives

Sunlit sea,
the drift of fronds,
and banners
of bobbing boats –
the seaside
of any day –
except: this
cold, bright body
of the fish
upon the planks,
the coil and
crescent of flesh
extending
just into death.

Even so,
in the distant,
inland sea,
a shadow runs,
radiant,
rude in the rock:
fossil fish,
fissure of bone
forever.
It is perhaps
the same thing,
an agony
twice perceived.

It is most like
wind on waves –
mere commotion,
mute and mean,
perceptible –
that is all.

Earth and I Gave You Turquoise

Earth and I gave you turquoise
   when you walked singing
We lived laughing in my house
   and told old stories
You grew ill when the owl cried
We will meet on Black Mountain

I will bring corn for planting
   and we will make fire
Children will come to your breast
   You will heal my heart
I speak your name many times
The wild cane remembers you

My young brother's house is filled
   I go there to sing
We have not spoken of you
   but our songs are sad
When Moon Woman goes to you
I will follow her white way

Tonight they dance near Chinle
   by the seven elms
There your loom whispered beauty
   They will eat mutton
and drink coffee till morning
You and I will not be there

I saw a crow by Red Rock
   standing on one leg
It was the black of your hair
   The years are heavy
I will ride the swiftest horse
You will hear the drumming hooves

Simile

What did we say to each other
that now we are as the deer
who walk in single file
with heads high
with ears forward
with eyes watchful
with hooves always placed on firm ground
in whose limbs there is latent flight

Four Notions of Love and Marriage

For Judith and Richardson Morse, their wedding

1

Formerly I thought of you twice,
as it were.
Presently I think of you once
and for all.

2

I wish you well:
that you are the runners of a wild vine,
that you are the roan and russet of dusk,
that you are a hawk and the hawk's shadow,
that you are grown old in love and delight,
I wish you well.

3

Be still, lovers.
When the moon falls away westward,
there is your story in the stars.

4

In my regalia,
in moccasins,
with gourd and eagle-feather fan,
in my regalia
imagine me;
imagine that I sing
and dance at your wedding.

Plainview: 1

There in the hollow of the hills I see,
Eleven magpies stand away from me.

Low light upon the rim; a wind informs
This distance with a gathering of storms

And drifts in silver crescents on the grass,
Configurations that appear, and pass.

There falls a final shadow on the glare,
A stillness on the dark, erratic air.

I do not hear the longer wind that lows
Among the magpies. Silences disclose,

Until no rhythms of unrest remain,
Eleven magpies standing in the plain.

They are illusion – wind and rain revolve –
And they recede in darkness, and dissolve.

Plainview: 2

I saw an old Indian
At Saddle Mountain.
He drank and dreamed of drinking
And a blue-black horse.

Remember my horse running.
Remember my horse.
Remember my horse running.
Remember my horse.

Remember my horse wheeling.
Remember my horse.
Remember my horse wheeling.
Remember my horse.

Remember my horse blowing.
Remember my horse.
Remember my horse blowing.
Remember my horse.

Remember my horse standing.
Remember my horse.
Remember my horse standing.
Remember my horse.

Remember my horse hurting.
Remember my horse.
Remember my horse hurting.
Remember my horse.

Remember my horse falling.
Remember my horse.
Remember my horse falling.
Remember my horse.

Remember my horse dying.
Remember my horse.
Remember my horse dying.
Remember my horse.

A horse is one thing,
An Indian another;
An old horse is old;
An old Indian is sad.

I saw an old Indian
At Saddle Mountain.
He drank and dreamed of drinking
And a blue-black horse.

Remember my horse running.
Remember my horse.
Remember my horse wheeling.
Remember my horse.
Remember my horse blowing.
Remember my horse.
Remember my horse standing.
Remember my horse.
Remember my horse falling.
Remember my horse.

Remember my horse dying.
Remember my horse.
Remember my blue-black horse.
Remember my blue-black horse.
Remember my horse.
Remember my horse.
Remember.
Remember.

The Fear of Bo-talee

Bo-talee rode easily among his enemies, once, twice, three – and four times. And all who saw him were amazed, for he was utterly without fear; so it seemed. But afterwards he said: Certainly I was afraid. I was afraid of the fear in the eyes of my enemies.

The Story of a Well-made Shield

Now in the dawn before it dies, the eagle swings low and wide in a great arc, curving downward to the place of origin. There is no wind, but there is a long roaring on the air. It is like the wind – nor is it quite like the wind – but more powerful.

The Horse That Died of Shame

Once there was a man who owned a fine hunting horse. It was black and fast and afraid of nothing. When it was turned upon an enemy it charged in a straight line and struck at full speed; the man need have no hand upon the rein. But, you know, that man knew fear. Once during a charge he turned that animal from its course. That was a bad thing. The hunting horse died of shame.

– from *The Way to Rainy Mountain*

In the one color of the horse there were many colors. And that evening it wheeled, riderless, and broke away into the long distance, running at full speed. And so it does again and again in my dreaming. It seems to concentrate all color and light into the final moment of its life, until it streaks the vision plane and is indefinite, and shines vaguely like the gathering of March light to a storm.

The Delight Song of Tsoai-talee

I am a feather in the bright sky.
I am the blue horse that runs in the plain.
I am the fish that rolls, shining, in the water.
I am the shadow that follows a child.
I am the evening light, the lustre of meadows.
I am an eagle playing with the wind.
I am a cluster of bright beads.
I am the farthest star.
I am the cold of the dawn.
I am the roaring of the rain.
I am the glitter on the crust of the snow.
I am the long track of the moon in a lake.
I am a flame of four colors.
I am a deer standing away in the dusk.
I am a field of sumac and the pomme blanche.
I am an angle of geese upon the winter sky.
I am the hunger of a young wolf.
I am the whole dream of these things.

You see, I am alive, I am alive.
I stand in good relation to the earth.
I stand in good relation to the gods.
I stand in good relation to all that is beautiful.
I stand in good relation to the daughter of Tsen-tainte.
You see, I am alive, I am alive.

Before an Old Painting of the Crucifixion

THE MISSION CARMEL
JUNE, 1960

I ponder how He died, despairing once.
I've heard the cry subside in vacant skies,
In clearings where no other was. Despair,
Which, in the vibrant wake of utterance,
Resides in desolate calm, preoccupies,
Though it is still. There is no solace there.

That calm inhabits wilderness, the sea,
And where no peace inheres but solitude;
Near death it most impends. It was for Him,
Absurd and public in His agony,
Inscrutably itself, nor misconstrued,
Nor metaphrased in art or pseudonym:

A vague contagion. Old, the mural fades ...
Reminded of the fainter sea I scanned,
I recollect: How mute in constancy!
I could not leave the wall of palisades
Till cormorants returned my eyes on land.
The mural but implies eternity:

Not death, but silence after death is change.
Judean hills, the endless afternoon,
The farther groves and arbors seasonless
But fix the mind within the moment's range.
Where evening would obscure our sorrow soon,
There shines too much a sterile loveliness.

No imprecisions of commingled shade,
No shimmering deceptions of the sun,
Herein no semblances remark the cold
Unhindered swell of time, for time is stayed.
The Passion wanes into oblivion,
And time and timelessness confuse, I'm told.

These centuries removed from either fact
Have lain upon the critical expanse
And been of little consequence. The void
Is calendared in stone; the human act,
Outrageous, is in vain. The hours advance
Like flecks of foam borne landward and destroyed.

Walk on the Moon

For Henry Raymont
21 July 1969

Extend, there where you venture and come back,
The edge of Time. Be it your farthest track.
Time in that distance wanes. What is *to be*,
That present verb, there in Tranquilty?

Headwaters

Noon in the intermountain plain:
There is scant telling of the marsh –
A log, hollow and weather-stained,
An insect at the mouth, and moss –
Yet waters rise against the roots,
Stand brimming to the stalks. What moves?
What moves on this archaic force
Was wild and welling at the source.

Rainy Mountain Cemetery

Most is your name the name of this dark stone.
Deranged in death, the mind to be inheres
Forever in the nominal unknown,
The wake of nothing audible he hears
Who listens here and now to hear your name.

The early sun, red as a hunter's moon,
Runs in the plain. The mountain burns and shines;
And silence is the long approach of noon
Upon the shadow that your name defines –
And death this cold, black density of stone.

Angle of Geese

How shall we adorn
Recognition with our speech? –
Now the dead firstborn
Will lag in the wake of words.

Custom intervenes;
We are civil, something more:
More than language means,
The mute presence mulls and marks.

Almost of a mind,
We take measure of the loss;
I am slow to find
The mere margin of repose.

And one November
It was longer in the watch,
As if forever,
Of the huge ancestral goose.

So much symmetry!
Like the pale angle of time
And eternity.
The great shape labored and fell.

Quit of hope and hurt,
It held a motionless gaze,
Wide of time, alert,
On the dark distant flurry.